DAFFODILS, *I pick for you*

DAFFODILS, *I pick for you*

JOLENE VANYO

PALMETTO
P U B L I S H I N G
Charleston, SC
www.PalmettoPublishing.com

© 2024 Jolene Vanyo
All rights reserved.
No portion of this book may be reproduced,
stored in a retrieval system, or transmitted in
any form by any means–electronic, mechanical,
photocopy, recording, or other–except for
brief quotations in printed reviews,
without prior permission of the author.

Paperback ISBN: 979-8-8229-4512-8

TABLE OF CONTENTS

daffodils 1
to wait for the spring 3
follow it 4
on painting 5
undress myself 6
mind the clock 8
home again 9
more ways than one 10
solitude 11
hesitation 12
time 13
another round for the pain 15
the united states of aesops fable 16
electioneering 17
politicians 19
politicians 2 20
fortune teller 21
somewhere else 22
el dorado 23
overcome 25
just around the corner 26
death 27
living 28
can you love 29
chasm 30
pretend we are home 32
anodyne to loss 34
landmine state of life 36
living without love 37
ode to hemingway 38

love is	39
love is, 2	40
the other side of losing	41
slowest of trains	43
pharmaceutical nation	44
denizen	45
Baltimore	46
back alley	48
at this stop	50
I'm listening	52
time loving tenderly	53
she was 101	55
love passed by me, blue	58
in unison we breathe	59
for my son	60
for my children, a grand canyon memory	62

((daffodils))

when living is a habit
a pattern without change
the dying is less tragic
just another face
another name
circle 'round the sun again
and wouldn't you know
it ain't comin' out today
but it's okay babe
I never mind the rain

so tell me where you're going
I'll tell you where I'm headed to
beyond the mountain there's a valley
with a river rushing through
among the foxtail and the clover
there are daffodils
there are daffodils

kneeling in the garden
dew drops stopping time
weed and clear the nettles
but thorns are all I find
I'd tell you not to worry babe
I know you'd lie and say the same
but I see those rain clouds
turning your eyes gray

so tell me where you're going
I'll tell you where I'm headed to
beyond the mountain there's a valley
with a river rushing through
among the foxtail and the clover
there are daffodils
there are daffodils

among the pampas grass and tamarisk
the road that leads us to
the sycamore the oleander
I'll be waiting here for you
in the sun-kissed meadow dancing
there are daffodils
there are daffodils

hold my hand
we'll lie together
the sky above us blue
among the hawthorn
and lavender
hearts tangled up in two
where dreams float up like stardust
there are daffodils
there are daffodils
there are daffodils
I pick for you

((to wait for the spring))

people will leave your life
in ways you never expect
some will depart, dearly
and some will drift slowly
away with a warm wind swept

the clatter of cups, the clink
of spoons, the staccato of the
cashier's ring
the man in the corner
clears his throat –
these are the ordinary things

the traffic moves outside the window
a passerby stops to tie a shoe
I consider the shadows and lights
that flicker on him,
when he stands again I see you

close my book, button my coat
leave the waitress a tip
reacquaint myself with the
weight of the day;
the clock keeps a steady tick

images appear and
memories return
at times you least expect
fractions of them fall like leaves
and you are left to wait for the spring

((follow it))

a star can fall forever
and be fine
we have learned how to collide particles
at such high speeds to render the knowledge useless
Hertz conducted his experiments in constant pain
from a bone condition his doctors could not understand
and now today his effort measures frequency
turn on the radio, tune in
you will hear the glorious efforts
there will forever be a pace of discovery
a high voltage discharged in a darkened room
and from it a spark will fall
we will follow it
and forever we'll be fine

((on painting))

apart from the scrape of knife against the grain of wood
and my own rhythmic breathing
there was no sound
there was only color
I cut my world in pieces,
unmoored a boat
untied a shoe
let slip the grip I had, refused
the promise of another
left the earth and returned
to relearn the art of living
on any kind of ground
when the land began to tremble
time shifted in my hand
the picture began to blur
and I heard
Pax vobiscum: welcome to paradise
this weightless fleeting hour
spent in a forest
painting a dream
while the trees around me burn

((undress myself))

the stories all begin the same way they end
love changes clothes between regimes
and mine lay bleeding
in a field of war in the land of dreams
bodies in carriage with hearts broken clock
the statesmen will lead you any way that you want
accounts payable, corpse on a shelf
to think that I set out,
I set out to undress myself

history pulses like an artery
pierced by perennial, incidental things
tragedy trickles out of circulation
and leaves a morgue full of this:
lips blue and faces stiff
bodies embalmed with bitterness
needing wings to get out
and I set out,
I set out to undress myself

far sunken are the sons of valor
beneath soil where daughters play
these proving grounds minted mounds
where generations give birth
only to detonate
where deities welded in our best sculptures
are mounted with intention to impart
the deathless one word lesson
they tell us: Love
Love with the will a captain has
going down with his sinking ship
float among bodies wondering
who can I help
when I had set out
I had only set out
to undress myself

((mind the clock))

mind the clock
it's later than you think
the eye that closes
opens the door to a room
where a rage of a dream is dancing
first a bolero, then a minuet
and finally a waltz
the room spins slower
around the composer
of an unfinished symphony
the notes molten lead in her head
drip solid into bullets
tick tock, *make it stop*,
make it go, send them all
smoking from the barrel
watch them ricochet off every shadow
glass breaks, silver is the sound
of the heart that aches
stone cold is the corpse
in the snow you turn over –
with the face of your own
with the soul of your lover

((home again))

my soul is tethered to a lonely place
pulled in by the wind and long grain
fields that whisper, bow and bend
in reverence to something
the impermanence of everything

I knew a little girl who dreamed of them
of running right through the thick of them
arms outstretched and eyes closed
bare feet sinking in the soft black coal –
soil so rich it feeds your heart
long after it has tended to the corn and oat
fingers brush by feathers tip
a silent splash in the ocean gold
while crickets hum their constant song
that drum with step toward endless horizon

I knew a little girl who saw that dream
pass by her window as she drove away
and I know a woman who sees it still
the dream that draws her home again

((more ways than one))

the heart can bend more ways than one
arteries wind like branches
crowded with blossoms
the breeze of you walking by
sends them all into bloom again
flush is my face with the petals that fall
the ease of you floating by
unaware of my presence
my soft steady beating
speeding up
leaves me wondering:
how long can the heart bend
more ways than one

((solitude))

solitude is my only home
erased from the walls
the ways that were known
fixed my best eye on a star, north
dreams are the only direction I roam

they tell me the nights are clear in Greece
close my eye and fly there
don't say hello to anyone I meet
unsteady as a madwoman
I stumble through the streets

the tarot cards have turned over the
hanged man
and that's not bad, she says
that's not bad.
but you're destined
to be alone in your days ahead

I smiled at her and said
Thank you: I understand

((hesitation))

for want of what seems
easy to create
harder to sustain
impossible to keep
a summer spent in hesitation
performing the liturgies of lingering
always more comfortable in between
the spectacle of being a speaker
of no one else's language
all the meanings as mysterious
as the sounds are crystal clear
mouth round and wide open
and still you can't hear
what it is I'm saying
and still I don't know
which way it is
I should be going

((time))

time, a great migration
a stampede of wildebeest
lit by the lions of years that chase
hours into days into weeks

time, a quiet ballet
a single dancer on the stage
tiptoes across the spotlight
off into a dark and empty age

time, it has a bedfellow
a friend called a sense of loss
they often walk together
and leave a trail of dust

it can disassemble your atoms
dissolve salt
lick wounds
it can make a flower blossom
or reduce a beautiful bloom
it can be both predator
and prey in your consciousness
make a blood bath scene and leave
you waiting in a mess

time, a book on a shelf
read once or not at all
time, the friend you never meet
or one you cannot recall

time, a beggar on the street
asking for more no one can give
time like money measured
between what is absolute and relative

time, the impatient driver
and the passenger half asleep
watching broken lines of a highway
blur together at higher speed

time, the eternity in a single blink
Chronos and Kairos in the sky
stars like jewels for centuries
shine so briefly in your eye

it can be a dredged-up memory
pulled from the sea floor
waves stealing
waves returning
all the sands to shore
it can be that which keeps
bodies afloat
in an endless rhythm ocean
exhale after inhale, repeating
and when the breath stops
time moves on –
right into another heart beating

((another round for the pain))

silence is my mother tongue
listening a matter of custom
yes sir I heard you
no sir I ain't dumb
though I may be a bit on that spectrum
just rather perfect my thoughts
leave my voice unused
not motor it around like you do
wasting gas
polluting a planet,
filling ears with wax
Came in with a book
took a beer for company
chose the stool at the end--
purposefully
not all girls who come to bars
want to leave with men
in fancy cars
and I certainly didn't come with a wish
for whiskey stench breath
to be blown in my face
at this unholy, unrelenting
unimaginable pace
good god almighty look at those lips flip flapping
jawbone jumpin' like a jack rabbit
semiautomatic mouth pounding words
in my brain, I am waiting
eyes rolled up like window shades
for rigor mortis to set in
tender give me another round for the pain

((the united states of aesops fable))

body politic and all the talk
of judicial remedy
every part stirs the pot to feed
the greedy belly
minister to the appetites
sapped of energy
by leaky bowels and a crooked crown
on a head that cannot see
these members of the body
cry out for mutiny
leave the mines, throw sickles aside
lift pitchforks to the sky
and what becomes of this
but a fool's twist--
for the foot that's never held a gun
fights the hand that cannot run
an artery without a vein
cannot contain the blood within
the kidney can live without its twin
but is at risk without a rib
a breast without hormonal link
is drained of all its milk
and the appendix, useless as always
flops around on the ground
wailing like a baby
a mouth disconnected from the brain
blows bubbles and drools away
and the brain without its mouth
can only think and never say
I know who did it
I know what was
the sustainer of this state

((electioneering))

carefully crafted podium deception
makeup men and hidden agendas
equestrian class horsemen
parading in fancy dress and false dimension
camera poised at perfect angle
dial in the lens, lose the edge
crop out the ugly and give out
the fuzzy
words
boil it down to a caption
provide a simple explanation
for convoluted, twisted
tenfold situations
what lies outside the frame
can be denied
what lies outside the frame
cannot survive
and what lies inside
is what lies what lies what lies
send the common man
to dig a grave in foreign sand
and build a cinematic backdrop
a primrose path for snapshot
sympathy
kings pose next to props
champions of, companions in
tragedy
let the news channel know
1600 Pennsylvania avenue
is calling at 2

get the grieving mother on film
saying thank you,
thank you sir, god bless you
Did you get it?
I did. Let's go
Let's roll out
a 30 second commercial
for Hugo Boss, Christian Dior
Chanel, Yves saint Laurent
some new scent
we'll call it:
What a nice man,
that Mr. President

((politicians))

of all the lines we live by
which words governed you?
there isn't a soul that hasn't stuttered
perhaps all language is a ruse

what are your parabolic parameters?
what is the length of the curl of your tongue?
do you let your sin masquerade as wind
moving in and out of a lung?

what is this operatic space you claim
where what you say is not what you hear
where oaths become a gilded curse
where shaking hands never means a deal

maybe these twisted sensibilities come
from loss of oxygen
perhaps you talk too much
perhaps you disembowel the constitution
with lawsuit after lawsuit

why don't you just stop, take a seat
go relieve yourself in the bathroom
wipe your mouth, that vestigial organ
close it, for once withhold yourself
from flinging words
like a monkey flings poo

((politicians 2))

rebirth this nation
or never come back
threats of death
promise of salvation
capacious terms
to jettison the framework
for another year of
spiritual disarmament
simulate happiness
digging a grave
chisel a tombstone
with a smile on your face
throw a nickel down
hoping I chase
getting real tired of this
melodramatic speak
this hidden lease liability
this gnashing of teeth
Geezus H Christ
if you're going to lie to me
deliver it more honestly

((fortune teller))

would you like to find yourself
see your future
in a deck of cards?
Shuffle twice
hold your hand over
this piled up stack of psyche
a cosmic garbage dump alights
she drew one out and spoke about
my dead lover
brought him back to life
all I could see in her one glass eye
was my reflection
and the difference between
apprenticeship and mastery
knowing when intuition ends
and becomes an enemy
she told me this was a summons
to overcome
the human condition
to be at peace and learn to love
your death that looms above
necromancy and other magic practices –
she said she's schooled in these
and by the way
that will be
80 dollars please

((somewhere else))

I always meant to be leaving
on my way to somewhere else
to find a country I can cry and
call beloved on my own
to feel a battalion of steel will
carry my bones
over tall fences, through grasses overgrown
well beyond the cemented passage
a place where body and mind converge in a fugue
and assume the position of necessary sleep
this search for home a false theology
I keep uncovering what doesn't exist
but I will keep looking as if
there is some god forsaken place
in this world I belong:
I never meant to stay here so long

((el dorado))

all aboard
the journey of no return
you, a machine
and all the other bodies
combusting
look out
see the ghost in the glass
you can't
recognize your own face
feel the train speeding up
you forget
your age
watch brick and steel turn over
to fields of grass
hills of clover
landscapes stacked
in the rear-view mirror
the lacquered edges of time elapse
every seat
has a screen
a ticket to ride
the theater of your own being
will you watch
or opt
to close your eyes---
do not.
or you will miss
the birds that emerge from clouds
and disappear into viridian ribbons

you will miss
the crack in the sky
that opens to sunrise
the light
that hits the church spire and
breaks into sapphire
you'll miss the sign, glittering indigo
neon that reads
next stop
el dorado

((overcome))

it was as though I finally broke
the habit of turning over
it's what the living do
orbit around planetary disgraces
until an unorthodox comet collides
and changes trajectory
self-implode, recover, then suitably repair
enough to call it
victory,
facile or fleeting
as it may be.
it's a good thing most of us
have conquerable souls
makes it breeze for the dealer
to sell
what it is you need to defeat
your Self
of course that comes
in either direction
recovery or addiction
maybe instead of
thousand-dollar therapy
island retreats, shopping sprees
and top-tier drugs
sit on a dirt floor and read
Invictus

((just around the corner))

truth is, we all need a guardian angel
not one that sits in clouds and wears wings
one that is found fleeting
in the faces around
it was her today
it is him tomorrow
if you lose sight of the sparkle
retrain your eye
she's dancing in the boulevard
he's wandering down the street
leaving a trail of promises
a lonely print of feet
so follow it
walk on, walk on
just around the corner
you'll find the love you seek
just around the corner
you are the one you meet

((death))

death is but the final blow
from a life of senseless beating
we throw the weakest in the ring
sound the bell for endless rounds
let the dogs keep closing in
see the bloody girls and broken boys
your neighbor, your cousin, your brother
these souls condemned to live a life
of unrelenting horror
and all the while the Great Contender sits
quiet in the corner
cigar lit, whiskey tipped, his eyes a flame a flicker
watching all, keeping score
patient is this stalker
he weaves among the crowd of men
who think they've cheated pain
men who shout like prophets because they profit
from the wretchedness of this game
while their money talks behind closed doors
where bets on heads are placed
In the end it's nothing more
than a petty useless trade
for a grave is the same for kings or slaves
and with time we forget every name
the gains will go to the man who knows
and nobody knows his way
can you tell me who
is the loser and who is the winner
in a world where every life ends?
we stand to raise the hand of
Death:
the one and only victor

((living))

living insists on persistent sharp edges
static transformers
jolts of electricity
synaptic waves undulating
in precise rhythmic order
the curator pauses at a portrait
adjusting the frame to make
a crooked smile straight
a bride tosses her flowers
while a keeper leaves a feeder for the bees
trees snake their roots
to chase the water factories take and
fractals in snowflakes
form and melt away
so we conjure up machines
to create the same
we pursue life perfect and we want
it to stay
perhaps the tube she breathes from
killed a thousand in the make
we grasp at any shimmer of life
ignore the ways we die in other rooms
sepulchered in waste

((can you love))

can you love without reciprocity
what happens when a false quantity of being is revealed
when pockets are empty
when relational detritus changes your personality
mildew in the museum of your hearts artifact
all the years can't clean
no longer can you give back
what you never once received
and you are left stumbling
for a switch in the dark
for the light to show
one of us is not human
and the other not
immaculately conceived

((chasm))

the wreckage is buried 10 years deep
we no longer dig for daggers or pillage for steel
we've learned to live atop
tangled wires and broken mirrors
we've come to know our terror back then was infantile
we reconcile
what we thought we knew
against the truth:
our youth
was full of shiny, delicate delusion
the sky was always falling and we fell through
clouds that opened and dropped down
to ground like bombs that blew
us apart
it wasn't the apocalypse
but it might as well been
for a while we thought
the tanks were driven
by a god too weak and a devil too cruel
but when the smoke cleared we saw
it was only me
it was only you
and a crater the size of a moon

things will never go back
to the way they were,
some say that's better
the grass will grow and the bones will mend
and I will send you a letter
from the other side of the room
just to say hello
how are you

we can still hold out a hand
over this chasm
we can still open our mouths
to whisper amen

((pretend we are home))

what has become after all these years
a tempered art:
the search for places that remember us
or maybe we embark
just to feel
the touch of skin again
to map out a face
like children exploring
fingers running along
jaw bone to lip
back up
to temple
wandering around
an eyebrow and down
to wipe out
a tear
with your thumb
even in the dark of night
you know as well as I –
there is no foreigner here
just a familiar space
within latitudes of change
gravity tossed by waves
ghosts holding on
to ropes letting go
of loss
of love
of longing
we allow the ocean to swallow
all borders

letting limbs drift along
with hearts in tow
the shores keep moving
out of reach
we land on an island
in between
anchor our bodies
to the naked unknown
let's just close our eyes
kiss awhile
pretend we are home

((anodyne to loss))

schrapnel scraps from a meteor shower
we thought we saw another form of life
born of lust, the maker's show just for us
lying on a blanket last summer's eve
I could have held you for another hour
I could have held you until the cut of moon
above your shoulder slipped down
into the crook of your collarbone
I would have plucked it with my lips
and let it melt on my tongue
I would have felt
the anodyne
to life, is love

what stood in the way
was a ledger
a balance of mocking birds
coming to collect a debt you never owed
how was I to know that would be
our last benediction of pleasure
stars fixed suspended quiet
before the high pitch of bullets stream
before your body heaved
before blood stained memory
made holes in a blanket
last summer's eve
we thought
it was schrapnel scraps
from a meteor shower

we found
it was the taker's show
and when death is near it feels like warm skin
and when stars fade they take a second blink
and the anodyne to loss, my love:
there is none

((landmine state of life))

how do we go on knowing
the days get shorter and the years desiccate
find yourself walking in a field of graves
don't be shell shocked at the atom bomb that awaits
this ordinary ordnance landmine state
of life
watch your step
first the tick, tock the last
death the blast
what did you expect from time, something more?
what did you want from this world, the savior dying
at your front door?
walk through the gallow of years
collect what sand remains
make yourself a castle
and if all you've got is a grain
close your hand around it
like an oyster, make a pearl
sooner or later your tock will come
your body will fly
your fingers unfurl
and you'll be free to release
your beauty to the world

((living without love))

what is love but cheap economy
a means to keep afloat
a penny to paddle away from the unknown
why can't you sit with yourself and be content, alone?
what is living but all bone and persistence
crawling in the desert to escape your own
prison created from wishes
what is love but a bridge of convention
in between moving clouds
fallible suspension
what is living
without love
but a more painful existence

((ode to hemingway))

bring me a cat in the rain
romance me in no small way
paint me a picture
my body your alchemy
play me a song
with words you can't find to say
let me watch you
carve my name in stone
take out your rope
tie a knot in my belly
and pull me close
pull my hair back tight
find my neckline with your lips
curl my toes with your kiss
breathe on me in dreams
so when I awake
cold and alone
I will have known
even the imagined love
is better than most

((love is))

kindness was in our job description
and we worked it
in our cute little aprons with ruffled hems
tight waist tied, highlighting hips
gypsum smiles gesturing for a tip
small talk while steaming milk
make a heart in the cup
and an art of delivering it
then turn around and whisper
we made fun of others, made fun of each other
stated the obvious
every now and then
Jenny would kiss Melissa
behind the counter and arouse
the positive and negative ions
among the customers
subliminal deposits
uncomfortable for some
titillating for others
a leisurely indulgence
like tiramisu
at 2 in the afternoon
ambiance imbued
with soft piped music
in the background
these storylines of women brewed
in the heads of men
in the café of youth
between the sips
where time is lost and
and love just
is

((love is, 2))

we brave wild seas to study
a creature we will never fully understand
spend decades watching its ways
pen tomes
stock libraries
obsessed is the world with the greatest of the unknowns
we peer with telescopes
we fly close
to flames and dance in rain
we pretend to own
build homes thinking it holds
up the walls, we post photos on
our thrilling encounters:
our silly smiling heads in the open mouth
of a beast about to chew us up and spit us out
I tell you the only thing it ever taught me
was how to stand after defeat
what is
love, love
is
a shape shifter
a silver-tongued speaker
that slips in at the funeral
and delivers the eulogy

((the other side of losing))

thought I couldn't lose when I bet on you
got coolered in the second round --
dealer had aces, I had crowns
took my last coin
slipped it in the slot
forgot you left home, decided not
to call you
held the phone
listened to the dial tone
drone on
got nothing left to give
nothing left to say
all we ever had we both spun away
put the receiver back
and wouldn't you know
two stools down a plumber's crack
pulls the lever and shouts JACK POT
I watch
three cherry rings and all the riches
spill at his feet
his wife stands up and screams
kisses him, ain't that sweet
I walk off alone
wind my way through smoke
and defeat
sit in the lobby
pen another poem
for the toilet bowl
trophy

so this is the consolation
prize, a sizeable volume of
knitted words, fabric to wrap,
sentences thread a silken sac
to hide the fat and
make it all more beautiful
does a butterfly emerge from every cocoon
or do you ever find one empty
what will emerge from dirt
where seeds were pressed too deep
to birth any kind of flower
maybe nothing
or maybe more letters
to cut and arrange
into words
into a plastic bouquet
of hurt
place it in the chapel
for the casino wedding at 3
watch the couples come out
drunk and happy
and wonder what it's like to be
on the other side of losing

((slowest of trains))

now I wear exit wounds
part and parcel of who I am
underneath all these overcoats
words caught in my throat
scars the mark of liberation
a celebration in nights of soundless weeping
I bleed but the blood does not leave
my veins, I hold it in and wait
for the slowest of trains
to carry me away

((pharmaceutical nation))

an aberration of the mind
preconceived equations run dry
and no matter the relation
we stick to formulaic math and lack
the needed imagination to
bring it back to life
let the record hide
the ways in which we tried
to break fibonacci's sequence
nature cannot be conned
into giving us
a spiral staircase
to everlasting happiness
maybe we should be more willing
to let things die
the clouds will always
have the last laugh
dropping rain on the day
we thought had no chance

((denizen))

routine as brushing teeth
every day at half past two
I walk past the smell of crude
oil, urine and wet paper bags
he sits like a barley sack
slumped like a heap of debris
on the corner of H and 17th
I wonder what twisted journey he took
to arrive at life like this
the world teeters on the edge of the same abyss
today I was full of compassion,
yesterday disgust,
and I am guilty of everything in between
someday he will disappear like the rest of us
I watch his gaze land somewhere outside of time
where all the years converge and the spirit
consigns itself
to waiting in line.
the weather has carved up his face
sun baked and eroded by rain,
thoughts fragment and wash away
while reason collects at his feet
he soaks up every sound of the city
and responds to none
pigeons peck at the dirt around
his real estate belongs to everyone
a fly lands on his cheek; he doesn't flinch
he wants to hear what it has to say
Have you lost your mind? it whispers
No sir, not today.

((Baltimore))

this city,
this city sighs
city of baptism and bunions
this ragdoll, mop-head, sopping wet city of
phlegm and faces on pavement crying
for mercy, begging for grace
pleading guilty in the
city of malfeasance,
negligence
and needles
city of broken glass hubcap switchblade scenes
city of knives and ravens, murder and surgery
blue collar white coat
board the bus
of subproletariat labor
and listen to a prophet
get a word in edgewise
listen to crackle and static
of police CBs and paramedic emergencies
city of profanity,
fines, tow yards, tin can alleys, brown bag wine
and yellow teeth
city of defeat
city of rise and shine
wind through the cobblestone streets
with scents of french bread and the stench
of sardines

city of murky water, fish rot and docks
where boats unload factory-made hope
youth imported holding tight to notions
of progress and their dreams
of saving an orphan
this city of blueprints and politician's plans
of storefronts and reconstruction
three piece suits with bulldozers
moving prostitutes with guns
this city of saxophones wailing,
a crooner closing her eyes
while a trombone slides
a sad note into the ear of drunken soldier
a city of tired souls and pearls in the gutter
a city of excuse me mister
a city of can you save my sister
a city of I'll try
a city of maybe,
maybe,
maybe I'll stay
just a little while
longer

((back alley))

tucked away
in the dead-end alley of an unmarked road
where houses lean on each other
like drunks going home, like their battered wives
waiting in the cold
holding up rusted pots
holding up tin cup chimney stacks
staggered in rows on the skyline
tucked away
where cats stray and crows land
on criss-cross wires, watching the boys below
fly off the ends of lumber-scrap ramps
with bikes they stole, eyeing the old man
on the balcony having his evening smoke
tucked away
in this fired-clay ruin,
in these piles of rubble and cobblestone
from cemented fissures and boarded up windows
sprouts a hidden bloom:
a curly-headed red on the third floor
steps out to remove
her laundry from the line.
unpins the moon, it clings taut to her skin
and winds around every curve
nearly naked bathed in white
throwing alabaster shadows and shimmers
of abalone –

hints of flesh every time she moves –
sending ripples and silhouettes and images
of wild things running wilder in the minds
of the wide-eyed boys below
who have stopped to watch her
for reasons they don't yet know
she tosses her mane as she heads back in
her beauty winks
the old man tips his hat and blows her a ring
the old man who's never left this street –
for the chance to see her
he's never felt the need

((at this stop))

I no longer feel
like bursting into tears
what a feat to be just fine here
at this stop after all these years
at this stop where the bus never appears
got on my vintage washed jeans
with slits in the thighs
a pack of bubblegum
and a sweater to keep me warm
I'll sit on this stump, twiddle my thumbs
pull out a book and eat my lunch
keep waiting for the ride that never comes
and I am just fine with that.
Just fine.
these days I am fascinated
by the bees at my feet
searching for flowers
I spend my best hours
watching birds chase each other
flirting with wires
traffic blows by in a medley of colors
and across the street
a boy kisses a girl and drops to one knee
a stranger next to me looks at them,
shakes his head and says:

isn't it sad we live in a land
where fifty percent of marriages fail?
I say to him: *maybe that means*
100 percent of people are happy
he laughs and walks off, I stay
and wait.
I guess for some
love is a bus
on an out of service line
you may think I'm sad,
but ask me
why I'm still smiling

((I'm listening))

some mysteries are better left alone
don't know if the trail I'm on goes home
but I'll roam until I die
through forests I know
but don't recognize
with a dog at my heels
a gun at my side
and when the night gets cold
I'll light a fire
lay my head on the ground
watch the embers glow, burn slow and grow
wings floating up to the sky
where stars catch dreams and release
all the memories inside
you told me time will tell
and I tell you
I'm listening
I've come to know from the quiet
time is a mystery

((time loving tenderly))

speak from the ages they have so much to say
write as if you are a hundred years deep
live as if you are sixteen
captivate my mind and then tickle me
the elders always know better or so I'm told
look at all these little young pine trees
saplings without any grease
just shiver and weep with their budding leaves
we have weathered the winter and more
the empty cabinets the splintered floors
we fell through each other
we punched holes in doors
to escape the fire we rolled over and over
and over
and with nothing left you plucked a piece of dry grass
ran it under my nose and made me laugh
so I say write as if you are a hundred years deep and
live as if you are sixteen
lend your soul some ink, let your gnarled hands speak
teach me the meaning of
time loving tenderly
choose your words carefully
And just when I catch you looking
so shaken and frail
reading some letter that came in the mail
you reach up poetically
and squeeze my breast
making sounds like a car horn
a flurry of slaps, a playful pinch
you wrestle me to the ground

and we are laughing again
despite the flat tires
despite no heat
despite the poor prognosis
and the steady beat
of rain on a leaky roof
I don't have to ask
what that letter says, I see it
in your eyes, one hundred years deep
I see it in the way you keep
getting up in the morning, lacing up
steel toe boots on tired old feet
bending over to give me
a kiss on the cheek, I see it
in the way you hold
my heart at sixteen

((she was 101))

a century sat in front of me
a monolithic pedagogue
delivering lessons with her eyes
deeper than any word she spoke
a voice following memory broke
time accumulating in a patchwork slur and
a crackle of notes
she won't answer the routine questions I ask
the information I need
a stamp on the official record
proof she's living
she doesn't care to tell
what she last ate
how well she slept
and how long has it been
since her last bowel movement
forfeit all protocol, she will only say
how they once kissed
behind an old granary
and they may have done more
had her father not come 'round the corner
caught them in the act, chased his boy
through the fields and
gave him a grand beating –
leather belt
pants down
bare naked as the day he was born
sun shining on places it had never been
yes ma'am that's how they did it back then
and as she watched him clench and scream

she couldn't believe
what a fine ass he had!
she laughed at this, then coughed
and laughed again
her eyes sparkled, she wasn't done -
I tell you, that's when I knew
Lord almighty I knew,
I better marry that man!
this time laughing so hard
she nearly hacked up a lung
reached for a tissue with a shaking
hand, knocked over a picture
on the nightstand and handed it to me
a sepia toned wedding photo
that's him, you see?
We were only 14 then…
married at 23…
and thick and fast as
the laughter came, it left
her gaze went wet
and retrograde
wandering out the window
covering vast territories
mapping out land so distant
it's rendered foreign
I looked around the room
at a time-traveler's remnants
silver spoons in frames
Werther's in ashtrays
pictures in albums

old hats old coats
china cabinets covered in dust
a grandfather clock with a swinging pendulum
lending the silence a rhythm
and the empty bed
made up and ready
for no one
I left all the questions
unanswered, she answered
the one I never asked instead
what is the measure
of living?
to hold the hand of those
that go before you
to hear the heart beat
with a memory
to let them speak
to listen before they leave

((love passed by me, blue))

love passed by me, blue
stopped to sit by the side of the road,
a stone's throw from knowing
how gravity goes
blackbird took flight and flew
with the threads of a sweater I spun for you
I watch it flutter away,
fascinated;
landscape stranger from this point of view.

love passed by me, blue
in the city with its dripping lights
alive at night with glass and knives
I wind through avenues of shuffling shoes
shiny polished shriveled and used
faces in the crowd suspended like clouds
study each one as I study the moon,
captivated;
it was you I never knew.

love passed by me, blue
in white sand sinks the orange hue
tangle my feet in seaweed green
and dangle my heart in the deep
while swells crash around the sound
of driftwood ochre to purple change
pick up a brush and begin to paint,
hypnotized;
blue is the wave love will break.

((in unison we breathe))

the morning bird will sing
to anyone who will listen
the visions will come
to the writers of fiction
even in age the body
is a testament:
when the mind still believes it
the limbs will pretend
the shadow on a wall
is a soul rising again
trees emerge
from cracks in the earth
and with quantum leaps
a nebula gives birth
to stars that plummet
into black seas
and beneath them all
the dreamers sleep
curled up in amniotic
fluid poised to breach
ready for the living
in unison we breathe

((for my son))

the distance between two points in time
has been measures in inches
mark the wall and mark off the milestones
with pictures
stitch the pockets they slip through
seams of memory that never seem to hold
I watched you grow
through the floor of a glass bottomed boat
marveled at the bluefin
yellowtail, discus, barracuda
all the schools you took me to,
all the pools of shifting shallow deep
to dark and shades of lighter blue
to think I colored you first
in my womb
never imagined
the hues you would introduce
I held your hand as you dipped a toe
sitting on the edge of sea meets horizon
wasn't ready to let go when you dove
and you went
head first
now I watch you from the floor
of this glass bottomed boat
swim through weeds, wander through reef

bring up coral constellations
gather nudibranch, lions mane, leaf sheep
I watch you, my proxima centauri
and the creatures you light
the stars you arrange in my eyes
like flowers in a cathedral
like water in a fountain, baptismal
with you in your ocean
I am
brought to life

((for my children, a grand canyon memory))

we found ourselves standing on the ledge
where winds trade secrets
and replace all we thought we knew
suddenly attune to all we borrow and lose
the gusts move clouds and carry our senses with it
while a thousand years collect in the pools
of our eyes and escape
through canyons in the corners out of view
here the light shifts the day
enters our veins and breaks
language falls away
and echoes translate
ephemerality
so we take what time we can
to sit awhile and witness
the river unfolding a universe:
a burial and a birth
a tired old man, sprawling out
his layered skin, sighing out
his last breath
that lifts a rock wren from its nest
sending it high to swoop and dive again
dancing for the first time
having just found its wings

www.ingramcontent.com/pod-product-compliance
Lightning Source LLC
LaVergne TN
LVHW092058060526
838201LV00047B/1454